ROGER FINCH

STATIONS OF THE SUN

Praise for *Stations of the Sun*
"Color, light, nature, and art in Roger Finch's poems
radiate an experience of miraculous attentiveness
to the power of desire and memory. Deftly musical,
the poems of *Stations of the Sun* find loss and hope
intertwined in affirmation, as time and changing
flesh become precise and eloquent words."
- James Hatch, Ph.D., Hunter College

Praise for Previous Collections by Roger Finch

"Full of exquisite craftsmanship...which insinuates
and inlays itself into one's consciousness."
- Ian Sansom, *Times Literary Supplement*

"All the poems in the book aim to enhance the
reader's aesthetic understanding."
- David Burleigh, *The Japan Times*

STATIONS OF THE SUN

Roger Finch

SOMERSET HALL PRESS
Boston, Massachusetts

© Copyright 2007 Roger Finch
Published by Somerset Hall Press
416 Commonwealth Avenue, Suite 612
Boston, Massachusetts 02215
www.somersethallpress.com

Cover Image: www.gettyimages.com
Cover Design: Herald Gjura

ISBN 0-9774610-3-3

Library of Congress Cataloging-in-Publication Data

Finch, Roger, 1937-
  Stations of the sun / Roger Finch.
     p. cm.
  ISBN 0-9774610-3-3 (alk. paper)
  I. Title.
  PS3556.I4564S73 2006
  811'.54--dc22   2006017942

CONTENTS

To my sister Merlyn

STATIONS OF THE SUN

BY NIGHT THE STREETS
OF PITTSBURGH ARE CANALS

If the lights inside his third-floor room
are dim enough, the observer
leaning from his window on one of Northside's hills
can imagine that the streets below
are dark canals. If the Barcarolle
from *The Tales Of Hoffman* is playing, he will hear
the black velvet water the music unfurls

lapping at the sidewalks; the glimmers
on glass that the harp suggests
will be scattered on the streets from steel-mill lights,
especially after rain, their long threads
scrawled through the cloth like silver. Sumacs
on the hillside he will interpret as palms,
influenced by Tintoretto's tinsel'd aigrettes;

he does not know yet that Venice grows
very few trees. When, his first night there,
seated among restaurant sterling and crystal
next to a real canal, the gondolier
breaks out in song as his sleek black swan
draws near, he recalls himself back home dreaming
of this place, water on stone turned to mother-of-pearl.

TO THE LAKESHORE

A bird I hold in my hands,
a bird beaded in turquoise
his wings and tail and crest quilled with black and white.
Uneasily he beats, as a hand-held heart
beats, but the bird's heart beats twice as fast,
two eighth-notes for every quarter-note of mine.
My fingers feel this clockwork, though it is soft-voiced

beneath his robe; they also feel
the pulse of his would-fly wings
lift in time with the lift of his breath against
the cage I am making with my hands. His eyes
drill me; quietly they countermand
my sentence. There were seven of them, kingfishers,
fledglings; one by one I threw them to the wind

and watched as their fans unlocked
stiffly and brusquely in the first rush
of updraft their feathers ever felt. I raise
this one, the last, and slowly unfasten my clutch.
He tests the emptiness and then breaks off
in a gust and clears the trees; he aims for the lake
but only makes the shore. That is far enough.

WHAT IS WRITTEN IN CLOUDS

Think how many times the sky must be reduced
to fit into the cornea
of the child wearing the red-and-gray
reindeer sweater who is lying on a hill
beneath it gazing up into it.
If its apparent diameter
could be measured, from one edge of the child's pool

of vision to the other, it would coincide
exactly with the largest
Imari charger held at arm's length,
the same cobalt-blue underglaze, the same cloud
motif. Anyone lying next to him
looking at his eyes would see the sky
as two small drops of Egyptian frit applied

to the enamel of his eyeballs, two sapphire
chips starred with the massed needles
called "silk" because of the clouds. The child
can see the plumes of foxtail grass at both sides
of the sky. You would see only a fringe
around the iris which might be his lashes
mirror'd there. He sees clouds piled into hillsides

that copy his own, top-heavy castles perched
upon them, full-rigged galleons
that will change instantly into dragons,
conventional things. He may even see mermaids,

witches, and basilisks, all those things
which could not exist before. Turn the scene
upside-down, the sky becomes lake and the birds

flying it fish swimming in it, his face at top
staring down into the water,
but without his reflection on it.
Turn it back the way it was. You may now decide
that his own face is the reflection
of an unseen watcher, the small image
of a pagan but very beautiful god.

RINGING THE WELL

In front of the house, grandmother's house:
The well, capped with a thick, square stone nicked
All over by the stonedresser's round,
   Whiskered with moss, tinctured with rainstain,
Couched in its coverlet of quaker—
   ladies, mint and gill-over-the-ground.

The feet of the child discover ring:
The tringle! trangle! of a thousand
Tiny triangles, the rattlesnake
   Zizz! zizz! of sistrums or the jingle!
Jangle! of tingle tambourine disks
   That whisk the well with the sound they make.

The stone, with its pins-and-needles fizz,
Its tinny titillation: a slab
Lithophone chiming like a celeste;
   Quick the feet tip-and-tap, tip-and-tap,
"Turn to the east, turn to the west, turn
   To the very one that you love best."

Then from the porch parents cry Danger:
   Stone may crack; well is full forty feet.
The child's mind, forever ringed around
   With St. Elmo's fire, sees himself fall,
Fall, head-over-heels, down earth's gullet,
   Alice greedily gulped underground.

All the way to China. Or further
          Flung Araby, where blooms the fabled
Incense Tree. The capstone cries "Eat me!
          Eat me!" – sudden board of gingerbread
Eager for ogre of Wonderland.
          The brain reels; body buckles; feet flee.

The after-after-noon: the long lull
          In the Lâlehzar, where tulips loll
Turbaned heads; the honeycombed tiltyard
          Of Chinese checkers with its petals
Blue and yellow and red; the harem
          Of Alcazar, all bolted and barred.

At the bottom of the well, bottom
          Of the well: lands, mysterious lands
Where the griffon and the dragon dwell.
          Hands, bewitching hands, beckon me there;
Only lack of pluck, lack of dare
          Hold me from falling beneath their spell.

WASHDAY

The laundry tubs are five midnight-marbly slabs.
They are always cool to the touch, as though lined
with black ice, the pith of glaciers that never melts.
Sheets left soaking in the crystal undersea
in them move at a touch with the kittenish grace
of octopus in their tanks in fish markets.
Now for a real magic act: the long ink-blue tress

poured from the Bulldog Bluing bottle twines and curls
among the sheets in the same pearly design
found in French endpapers, but it does not dye
the white sheets blue; instead they are more brilliant
than before. When Mother hangs them in the yard,
they flap their great albatross wings, clean bunting
for a mountainous country perpetually attired

in snow. What flag could be more appropriate?
The spaces between their snapping sides are rooms
for disembodied people. Mother's nightgowns
and Father's pajamas waltz together, a ball
for the newly convalescent, but without heads
or arms or legs, dancing with the abandon
of unearthly angels high among the clouds.

THE CAT LADY

The 8-carat cat's-eyes flare out
    from the pile of long white rabbit wool
    in her lap. Our own patchwork streetwalkers
have gone to their corners. She is telling Mother
she crocheted a tablecloth from sewing thread
        "so fine you could ball it up
in the palm of one hand," for her newlywed

son's wife. "Later," she tells us,
    sipping at the tea in her saucer'd cup,
    "I found it in her cellar, black with soot."
Her indignation stiffens the pug-nosed mask
on her waterless satellite as her guesswork delves
        in our coal bin for remnants
like this. Mother has already lined our shelves

with the canned goods this woman's cheques
    will buy as soon as she finishes
    her portrait. The tea-cakes gleam with real
crushed garnets, nothing must go amiss. I purr
and shoot my 12-carat gems toward a new chat.
        I am a precious silent film star
but still a son, clearly no match for the cat.

THE BEAR WENT OVER THE MOUNTAIN

Father, dear Father, why did you always
    sing The Bear Went Over the Mountain
all of a Sunday morning, just as you shaved?
You startled us, Santa Claus at the bathroom door,
    your beard whipped from scraps of soap you saved.

The big, soft, badger-hair brush whisked up its curds
    (so like the head on a glass of beer)
and laid it around your oxbow mouth as it went
on woofing through its froth of mad-dog madness,
    "To see-e what he-e-e could see." You would peer

in the mirror and popeye at us, watching
    us watch you, and your voice would bull out
to come down on the punch line: "He fell into
a dark hole/ And covered his arrrse with charcoal,"
    as we folded in giggles. A shout

would ascend the stairs, "Wil-l-liam" – that was Mother
    listening up from her Chopin *Barcarolle*,
meaning, "Don't use that word in front of the children."
Why did you go over the mountain so soon,
    dear Father, and fall into your dark hole?

DOOR-TO-DOOR SALESMEN

Mother could not resist them.
They came in with their smiles, their vinyls,
their stainless steels, and sat in our side chairs.
Colors no rainbow mustered fanned in their laps;
our interest fanned with them. Our first ballpoint gleamed
in the wanderer's hand, sleek,
reedy, projectile. He had other wands. His knack

made sterling silver appear
on our table; porcelain, crystal;
whole encyclopedias filled our shelves.
No one house can hold all their magic. It spreads
from lifetime to lifetime. With their dark blue suits,
their smiles, their warm hands they come
and knock on my door. I can not resist them

THE MUMMY'S GHOST

Think of the most exotic woman you know,
    Persian, or Peruvian, or a blend,
so many shades of blood that nowhere in the world
    is anyone like her. Think of her,
now, sitting there, a silver streak in her hair,
and she might be Nefertiti. The make-up man
    will have given the same arch to her brows,
    the same curve to her mouth, the same cast
to her skin. As the movie moves on, her mind
    moves back to the XVIIIth Dynasty.
    You know that when the curator burns
        tanna leaves and reads the words
    off the ancient papyrus that he found,

the mummy will revive. The smoke from the leaves
    still blackens his study and the sound
of the last few words have not escaped his lips
    when a crash! of glass off in the night
warns that the mummy is here. Real screams go up
from every childish mouth as a hand comes in
    and eyes glinting through the winding sheet
    follow. That woman in your room stands,
turns, walks down the hall, straight into the mummy's arms.
    As they go her hair turns white, her face
    shrivels, her skin shrinks, and she goes on
        getting older as they go
    from the movie straight into your dreams.

SODA FOUNTAIN

That is Albert behind the counter in hospital whites.
We call him "soda jerk" and laugh, for he is not smart.
He hangs his paws over the marble and bites

at our banter, but very gently. His rampart
harbors Renoir's muted colors in old glass;
he is trained to squirt his efflorescent art

across the plainest ice creams; his syrups mass
in formation, ready to transfuse rainbows
into our afternoons. I come to the impasse

where he rules and amorously I disclose
his name. I cool my palms on the waxy stone.
The lifeguarded body I have seen him expose

in locker rooms is one long erogenous zone
beneath his virgin's costume. He asks what taste
I want and shows me his palette. I want bone

lubricated by the sun, muscles braced
by shadows, skin turning into a lustrous blend,
strong mouth against my mouth, arms around my waist.

I order the sweet, warm flavor of a friend.

THE MOON SEEN THROUGH THE SUPERSTRUCTURE OF HIS *SYMPHONIE ROMANTIQUE* PLAN

Two-fifths of it would be Berlioz
in a Bristol royal-blue glass decanter
   in the form of a crown; one fifth more
would be Debussy, in the cloudy pale blue
opalescent glass of Lalique, a muffled blend
   of jasmine, orris and gardenias.
Three floors below lay the tangled upper end

   of the "garden" vibrating with moonlight.
The rest cascaded in brambles down the hill,
   as the famed gardens of Babylon
were imagined by Maxfield Parrish. Never mind
that it is largely thicket, briers, long spears
   of rushlike grass: it is dark and June
and there are conspicuous roses. One hears

   possible crickets hidden in their castles.
About midnight IRON CITY BEER an Ondine
   will appear near the wild-cherry tree
and will dance as they dance in *Lilac Garden*
(Ravel's *La Valse*) in a three-quarter-length silk skirt
and with soft TIME 10:00 gestures. The clock
strikes 10. The audience sits; the lights dim; the concert

   begins. *Adagio*. Violas, muted,
tremolo, hovering over a bass clarinet,

French horn IRON CITY BEER and two bassoons
in their velvety register. The cellos,
divisi: the first desk makes short, chirping clicks
   high upon the A string, while the rest
exude shimmering TIME 10:01 harmonics.

   Suddenly the harp begins the count
from one to twelve, in stopped notes, and violins
   rustle, whisking dry leaves of oboe
dizzily upward IRON CITY BEER Here I may
either mix in the nasal bellwether throat
   of an English horn, or three muted
trumpets to mirror the moon and make it float.

TOURISTS SEE HIM SHAVE

Our apartment is at the head
of Memorial Bridge. Bay windows lean
out over traffic, Virginia leans its shores
against the bellies of the windows.
The batiks he bought in Baltimore
have turned the room into a tent;
creatures carved from jade and flowers with gold veneers

contend from backgrounds of wild
disagreeable colors. The patch
that overlooks the Potomac's palmy fronds
is always open; only the walls
have curtains. We are painting the bathroom
purple. It is pure oil paint,
dries slowly. He shaves in the front room. He stands

at the fireplace, shaving mug
on the mantel, and consults his face
in the overmantel mirror. The second floor
is eye-proof. A double-decker bus
rounds the bridge and forty tourists gorged
on cherry blossom views stare
at a naked half-god throned in lacquerware.

BIRDS IN THE ATTIC

Dispossessed, I move house into my workroom
above the antique shop. My belongings stack
in one corner. A door with brass lion's legs
   is my bed. I have other riches.
   My hair is amber. The static stored
in each strand picks up small chinks of goldleaf thrown
from half-gilded frames. Even my ears, those two flared

orchids, capture golden beeswing in their throats.
At night, as my board or beast carries me flat
above an ever-closed opening into sands
   painted by Rousseau, fumes from the size
   glaze my skin and by morning my face
is a highly-flecked liqueur. There is a skylight
in the stairwell, way for stars to step through glass.

Birds roost on the roof, though, and the glass is fogged
with their whitewash. From time to time, a wind-swept
Orpheus drops into my underworld, wings
   whisking the air into eggwhite froth
   and more goldleaf, clouds of it. One night,
as my face slowly turns to Tutankhamen's mask,
my head will grow a hawk, its eyes mildly moonlit.

A HOMING INSTINCT

As I entered your seventeenth-century house
I knew that at last I was home. My eyes reeled
with the shock of recognition but my heart
stepped in, as comfortable and confident and right
as Cinderella's foot was in its clear-cut
slipper, truly the only one that would fit.
The fireplace cried "Light me!," the furniture cried
"Touch me!" Beneath my gaze the amber glaze of chairs,
tables, dressers, chests, began to spark and glow
as amber flickers when rubbed through hair, as a soft
tabby cat sparks, in dry weather, stroked at night.

In the stone room I settled in. I was there
to stay, I thought you assumed that. Above our heads
hung a viking's hoard in pewter; the beams were old,
smoky, scarred, but they held the weight. This was far,
far too much for one man to have. You were less
the keeper of all this beauty than an expert
guest. We could share your life. We did share your marred
genius, plotted a play together, shared fits
of laughter, your real genius, your need to charm.
My presence was perfect; we might have lasted long
there, but misgiving, yours or mine, took us apart.

I fear for the new residents of that house.
They will never own it. Our love is too strong
to keep away from it. Neighbors say you failed
because you wasted money, your time, your life;

your friends say you failed because you failed to use
the talent they were sure you had. My one thought
now is that the house maintained your unconfined
flair for living, just as it visibly expressed
it. I feared that if you left it would kill you,
though I pretend that our hearts will one day meet
on that cold hearth, basking in their own firelight.

AN EXHIBITION OF PRIMITIVE PAINTINGS

The early eighteenth-century walls
antedate the artist's memories
    by two hundred years.
Her barnyards and sleigh rides borrow the limelight
from rafterfuls of pewter; their tin outshines
    the artist's side-show in Old-World magic.
        Yet, the paintings are "right" here.
Their flat eye-blues fuse in the decanted gloss
from woodwork; their unblinking enamels fire

    to the mellowness of Sandwich glass.
    Buddy has promised only sunlight
        and candles; his heart
has enough thunder to make the quiet places
crackle. I scatter loosestrife and goldenrod
    into anything that will hold water;
        the fireplace bristles with a mound
of hay fever. The artist curtsies in the yard
in Doulton dress. The clink of sherry is donned

    by hand after hand as guests arrive.
    A silver ghost discharges two toys
        as their lords step down
in old Hollywood attire among the guinea hens.
Visibly they make their rounds, dueling the soirée.
    Second to everyone, I circle
        with trays of fire for their flaunts.
I cannot buy one small slice of a way of life
recalled, but my own memories are brighter than paints.

FIRST FLIGHT

Fly British Airways.
    One stewardess has apples
    in her cheeks. During meals-on,
  unaccountably, I begin to cry.
I am going home, I am going home, I chant,
but it is not home, it is my grandparents' home.
    The empty seat beside me is Mother's.
She often dreamed of this trip. I take her hand,
    "Soon, soon," I whisper. The change in time

sends me to my bed
    minutes after I arrive.
    The big black cabs, the gaslights,
  were too much magic for one night.
I am amazed that millions of people live
this magic. I sleep as one drugged, visualize
  the world around where I have landed.
Morning, and the sky flutters in. I gaze out
  and England, England waves in my eyes.

IMPRACTICAL JOKES

On our way back from dinner,
  Buddy and I draw *Kilroy Was Here*
    on a subway ad.
The third man, a mild-mannered man, prigs and smugs
  at us. He disappears into the car
ahead of us. Before it is time to get off,
  he gets off, arrives at our hotel
before us. The room key is inside. He ducks

  beneath the covers, feigns sleep,
   though we trip-hammer the door. "No one
    falls asleep that fast."
We rouse a Dickens Jew, complete with nightcap,
  from the room next door. He brays at us.
"Is your dance card quite filled?" we ask the closed door,
proceed to fill his breakfast request with yoghurts,
  eggs-over-lightly, orange juices, ham.
Clearly we are still the jokers of our class.

WE TAKE THE RAIL ROAD

On the way to Aberdeen
the train slants through sunlight as sparkly as ale.
Villages are barnacled to cliffs
beneath us to break our fall.
Sheep safely graze on moss on the highland half,
the steepest country in the world.
We whiff the air, look down. The sea stands stiff

against the coast, its white crown
flashing. We pass the turf wall the Romans built.
Like an army of southerners camped
on the moors, my heart falls sick.
I watch the seabirds release their hold on the hem
of the land and wonder if they
are used to it or as delirious as I am.

NEGLECTED GARDENS

My garden was made of stone; hard and precise;
  it was set with the rarest jewels
in the plant kingdom. I had seventeen sorts
of campanulas, some so fragile that their stems
  were needles, and each species iris
named in the catalogues. Your garden was coarse,
loud, rank; a wild hillside patch fenced in with mesh
  to keep out chickens; a yearly vein
of new bulbs that yielded spring's bright motley ores

and then collapsed in a snarl of weed leaves.
  My garden was wrested from a stand
of equally unkempt daylilies. When I left,
the daylilies rallied in revenge and choked
  the pampered foreign darlings. Rogue seeds
from nearby hedgerows spread through their ranks like deft
cancer cells tramping through the flesh. In two years,
  out of order came chaos; the chaste
exactitude I worked was effaced; bereft

by my absence, the garden mourned me with madness.
  When you left, your garden went unchanged;
it managed to regenerate itself; its wealth
of color scarcely diminished, in fact grew
  bolder and more brilliant every spring.
Some day a gardener must thin that bed. Life needs breath,
and those untamed outlaw flags will suffocate
  if allowed to spread in waves that way,
seeming to signal or celebrate your death.

HOW TO GET FROM HANEDA
TO THE HILTON HOTEL

The cab driver is intent
on hurtling himself against the seventh fleet.
     He rolls down the window,
   jack-in-the-boxes his head out. He yells
to a taxi friend. "I've got a live one here,"
he seems to say, meaning I did not tell him
     where I want to go. I am a doll,
       bolt upright in the back, eyes
glued to "open." He could take me anywhere

     he wants, and does, mile after mile
of twisting elevated highway through junk.
     First impressions count,
   and I am counting: from zero down
to minus one hundred, minus one thousand.
It is ugly, ugly, ugly. This is not the wheels
   talking, it is me, a litany,
     please, please take me out of here.
This madman is my Virgil; he is the hound

   with three heads. America
is back there. This is my new home. I am far,
     just as far from both.
   Finally my tongue uncleaves. I speak
my first Japanese, an ugly sound. At last,
we land. Luxury, quaintness, elegance erase
   that first frightening taste; but nothing
   can erase disappointment.
I left behind everything that I love most.

A BETWEEN PLACE

"…in Zoroaster's own teachings
concerning the hereafter,
…there were three abodes,
Heaven, Hell and a shadowy between-place
for the morally indifferent,
whose inhabitants knew neither joy nor pain,
but merely existence."

- Mary Boyce

I board the train called Money. All of the trains
are called Money. The crowds are packed in so tight
they cannot move. Some of the people have died
but they will not fall, they cannot move. The train sways left,
and the crowd crams to the left; the train sways right,
and the crowd crams to the right. No one cries. A wheeze
is squeezed from them. Like an accordion knifed

in the lungs, no music comes. Kokeshi dolls
are meant to be the souls of dead or unborn
children, a collector told me. He showed me cribs,
chests, bins, caskets full of them. They did not move
even when shaken, they were wedged in so tight.
Painted-on eyes peered out from newel-post heads.
If the dolls are souls, where do the bodies live?

THE LOOK OF THINGS FROM
A 2ND FLOOR WINDOW

The houses of 3 o'clock in the afternoon
are haunted by the perpetual neon glow
of soap opera. From time to time a wave
of white passes behind a frosted window.
The street is deserted. It is solemn, grave,

trying hard to be a better neighborhood.
No one ever lingers in it. People pass
through it, have addresses which do not include
it – for it has no name – but never look through the glass
of its eyes. No footsteps break its solitude.

I do not see a girl dressed in a light green
sweater, blue shorts, long black stockings. I am not
going to see a thin old man in a wheelchair
pushed by a girl in a Catholic school dress. What
I do see is a plain gray street, basic, bare

even of pigeons. If there is a dirty white dog,
he's been dying for the past three weeks, and no one
comes to comfort him. Across the world's crevasse
there is America, where people stand in the sun,
and in cricket-bristly twilight mow the grass.

DOLLS DO NOT DIE

Each doll has three men in shadow black
    to work it. Only the man
  who operates the right hand and the head
  is barefaced; the other two have hoods.
It is the foot-man, whom I have seen backstage,
    who walks the woman to her death,
love suicide. She writhes in blood along the ledge,

    courtesy of the left-hand man. Her breast
    beats with a hand, moments past
  her agony. The way to make her
  seem to die is take away the hand,
but her player cannot withdraw from the throat
    of death, her ecstasy. Love
is that fisted thing inside that makes her hurt.

PUERTA DEL SOL

We group for a photograph
   in front of this Moorish battlement
My ladies rustle like a railing of dolls
cut from tissue paper. I am a sun god
   My rays zigzag from around my head.
We had a photograph at home, Uncle Miles
   and I flanked by a long arcade of aunts,

   I a replica of him
   in summer white, without the moustache.
My past is now more mysterious than his.
Someone's child will wonder who this Sharpless is
   perched against the age-oranged stone, onion arch
haloing him with dark. He will not notice me
   bend toward one woman's neck, my one wish

   to bite the spine out or pin
   a spur through the nape, letting clockwork
spurt. The child might expect me to flash my hand
on high, the white fan in it flared like a wing.
   He would be shocked to see his mother slump
in front of me, her stuffing suddenly gone,
   my fiery face feeding on her wick.

GRECO'S HOUSE: THE GARDEN

When I think of Spain, I do not think of bullfights
    and flamenco; I do not think of saints.
I think of a small white flower, perhaps jasmine;
I think of cats drowsing in a spoiled rock wall;
I think of sunlight, sunlight on dust,
sunlight on the raw brick earth, sunlight on cats;
and night, night with stars in its spire. I can taste

that night: clear; leafy; metallic. I think Spain
    and this garden comes to light; not grand.
Where is its showiness? Raw-brick brown, slate, white.
In such a garden, garments are flowers; its guests
    carry the seasons. Hollyhock red
yields to larkspur blue; a skirt lifts and lilies
appear. An artist whose skies are far more glad

with angels than his garden is glad with paints
    might overlook its small sweet outbursts.
His dark parts are near the ground. If there are blooms,
they are meant for the altar; the viewer tries
    to peel them from the wall. The half-nudes
that root and gaze up have skin the same brick-brown;
they do not have wings but they feel as light as birds.

WHAT IS WRITTEN IN LIGHTS

The evening air turns, turns
    purple, then bronzes. The sky
  behind the Puerta del Sol grows rich
as the flag of a new African nation.
The Moorishness is everywhere overmapped:
    rose canes grow in arabesques,
the grillwork on windows quote something in script

from the Holy Qur'ān.
    The lights along the Calle Mayor
  imitate those named stars that now burn
into view. In the albedo of cafés,
tables spindle and strut; human legs are thinned
    to walking sticks. Profiles are the kings
on postage stamps, toward the addressee half-turned.

FLAMENCO DANCER

Her face is powdered with lacquer.
  Her eyes, borrowed for the evening
From a duke's opal ring, clatter
In their bezels. Her hands are pleating
The air. Her skirt's starched fans shatter
  As she shakes them, petals gleaming.

Her shoulders stretch up two adders
  Or flamingos' necks. Her fingers
Flicker at us; their bills chatter
  Fast as firecrackers. Her stingers
Arch, ready to strike; she hammers
  With her hands and sends down splinters.

If her body were a glance, slashes
  Would outline us in a knife-thrower's
Trick as she lifts the eyelashes
  Of her dress at us and glowers.
Her heels fire their lightning-flashes
  And our chests go red with flowers.

ROSE GARDEN, ØSTRE ANLÆG

Roses clamber over the arbor
  around me. They make the filigree
of brambles around the majuscule
  in an illuminated manuscript.
I am not an Irish saint in sackcloth,
  his comma eyes turned down as though heaped

with the world's woes, and I am not a virgin
  with a unicorn's head in her hap,
and yet, seated in this uncial cave,
  the sun powdering with gilt my face,
I am at the opening of a page.
  On the green in front there is a mass

of monthly roses: pink, yellow, peach.
  I note how the abundance of one hue
sways the eye; I note that chains are used
  to swag the climbing roses from post
to post. Already I plan to match
  this garden; I see it reproduced

on my own land, though I may not be back
  for years. How quickly do roses grow?
Patient as a saint, I feel my powers
  coax the canes out of the past.
I imagine a ghostly garden
  tended by an older me, no ghost.

PICNIC AT KU-RING-GAI

We drive through a woods
    designed for a Beckett play.
    All the trees are one: *Eucalyptus.*
    This could be home. I cannot believe
in the ranginess, though, the dustgray oak-tag
    skewered on wires. Nothing real
happens here. The men of *kendo* club slave

for us. They pitch camp,
    build a fire, and soon gray smoke
    is matching its trees. What is that shrieking?
    Not shriek, but laugh. A kingfisher sways
on a branch, big bird. "Kookaburra," one man says.
    It crows down, sweeps up our crumbs,
a flash of gray-blue against gray-brown. The men propose

a game of softball.
    The two slim Japanese girls
    are too well-dressed to play. From sidelong
    they eye those shaggy bears. Like bear cubs
the men romp, shout "Catch!" and "Run!" The girls wry
    their mouths. They have no taste for this.
Delicately we chew that language without verbs.

THE ANCIENT SEAT OF KENTISH KINGS

The sky was rounding its shrill November winds
the way we rounded the city walls that round
the city, headlong and laboriously,
struggling to surmount the great inverted bowl
of gusty force that blared fiercely and hoarsely

through a clattering string symphony of trees,
It was assuredly the wrong time to come:
the old Norman walls that blossomed biscuit brown
so explicitly in the "Pride of Britain"
Guides were now gray as granite, a granite town

brayed beneath a sky set with flint-gray cobbles.
But once inside that forest of fragrant stone,
Canterbury Cathedral, whose pearly wings
glimmer like wood doves as they unfan in their
feathery lofts, whose reeded trunks have yearly rings

encrusted with flowery cameos of light,
we walk an Aladdin's garden, where jade trees
bloom rose quartz and amber, and kingfisher's quills
vine their robe-of-Mary blue forget-me-nots
up the bell tower and over Heaven's sills.

WHAT IS WRITTEN ON THE WINDOW

Spring rain. The windowpane mirrors the luster
of bezoar, that rain-relinquishing stone found
in the belly of some animal "like a sheep
or goat," the adhesive sheen of snail-silver,
redundant dew on the satiny background

of hollyhock petals. The child's face inside
the window's veil is an 18th-century
finial in the shape of a fruit, pickled
with mercury and awaiting its final
laying-on of gilt. Outside, an apple tree

is blooming from its famille noire underglaze;
its complexion is derived from manganese,
its iridescence from the pearls of rain
that blister on the mother shell and then run
down through the long nodular capillaries

of Mongolian script. The child practices
what a Japanese artist did to paint bamboo,
transcribing into ink its moonlight-outlined
shadow on the shoji. I have real paper
windows now, where the imprint of pine seeps through,

and knobby plum and bony bamboo, the three
"auspicious salutations." I would welcome,
though, the candor of glass and the polychrome,
luxuriant – if somewhat too wordy – pattern
of apple trees against the windows of home.

VIEW FROM A WINDOW AT TAKAYAMA

Manet's eyes would have leaned down, as my eye leans,
through the window's slats onto the scene below,
"umbrellas in the street." He would have painted
the slats. They are important. They make the surface
of the painting coincide with the fine-grained

surface of the canvas; they stress the near-round
form of the umbrellas; they provide tension.
Most of the umbrellas are black. This, too, is important.
They point up the occasional greens, browns, coral reds.
From time to time a single head, unadorned

but with a wimple of beetle-shiny hair,
appears in cameo against the black silk
shell of the umbrella; better, yet, two lovers.
Against the harp-string tautness of autumn rain,
their ivory bodies would have the softness of furs

against cut glass, mirrors, crystal chandeliers.
That is why, when I speak of the man across
the table, I will observe how delicate
his lashes are, as filmy as their shadows
on the brows of his cheeks, will note how they melt

or seem to melt as the steam from his teabowl
lays its lacquers on their threads, just as I have seen
the wood of his flesh turn to pearl in the agate
breath that rises after the bath, and have touched
his skin with my own wax skin as he gleamed like that.

WINTER SUNLIGHT, SUMMER RAIN

Think of the things you can never have,
    stroking your sister's apple-gold hair,
drowning with a friend in the yellow-diamond
    glitter of operas, undressing
        before the gilt-framed, firelight-filled
mirrors of high Victorian rooms so long
    as you stay here. Nothing you have recalled

    will be found here. You inhabit towns
    your mother never heard of, you dwell
in buildings your friends will not visit; your face,
    even your face, as you glimpse the skin
        of it skimming the storefront
windows of jadewrights' shops, seems to have been slipped
    from the backing of the past. You paint

    your winters with the peacock-colored
    lacquers of porcelain-spired cities
in the South, as opposite as possible
    to your homeland's winter white. The sun
        glinting on it imitates
those massed needles in sapphires and other gems
    called "stars." Summer, by contrast, results

    in witchcraft weather: the endless dark-robed
    days that cannot be cast out by spells,
days that with their windmilling familiars, crows, trail
    the sky, their eyes turned on the mouse's

hole, the lair of the vixen.
Only at night will the magic work, as handclaps
bring on the sleeper the skull-white rain.

THE BAT TREE

From far away, it is as if the great,
baggy chandeliers in a palace in India
had their crystals replaced with jet or muffled
with crêpe in mourning for a rajah. Young monks
    in marigold robes walk out and stir
the velvet evening-bag bodies from the trunks

of the trees upward through their bare ribs,
making Hallowe'en of New Year's with the flags
of their bodies against those chittering clouds
of Spanish fans. Through the camera's sharpest lens
    I see the glittering crystal stamens
around their noses, the recurved cyclamens

that line their ears and the mussel shells
that are the outer skin of them. If you look close,
you will see they beat very like the human heart,
opening and shutting their wings with every breath,
    as the heart does when it has love's smoke,
or when it drinks the final dark blood of death.

AT HAEIN TEMPLE

(Historical Site and Scenic Place No. 5)

Its very New England trees
and their nearly-New-England clerestoried dark
might feasibly have served out own childhood's God,
resp. Protestant and Catholic. We should
   have, then, sighted some gold cross of Him
   hanging in its stellar-vaulted chancel
where there was none. We did find a matching dim,

   voices-held-below-a-whisper
awe-full hush in its natural silence: birds
held their song in the birdfooted branches; acorns
refused to drop through the squirrelless shadows. Ferns,
   only ferns, retained their ages-old
   gestures, but faintly, making no more
sound than candlebuds quivering in the hold

   of their rubyglass vigil palms.
Hardly surprisingly, the silence was not
natural. Some ghostly arrival touched me and
my northernlighted aureole came on, with bands
   of orange and purple. It was odd
   how fully I came afire, walking
hand-in-hand with a beautiful foreign god.

Seoul, May 1981

THE ROPE DANCER

Five o'clock in the morning.
Broken wings are beating against the pavement.
    A cat has caught a pigeon
  or one of those gray-and-white magpies
  I have seen nesting in the sago palm.
  I rise, look out. A young man in shorts
is skipping rope. From his measured pantomime

    he stares at me. Even through glass
I smell his rich stink and I begin to sweat.
    Back in bed, I count the stanzas
  of his poem. He is skipping rope
  for me. The next morning, I slip out
  on the balcony during one of his rests.
I must have something to do, so I promote

    an old vice, have a cigarette.
As he jumps, as I lounge there and smoke, we gaze
    at each other. Day by day
  we grow skillful. Our courtship consumes
  the daybreak hours. Through the fumes, I dream
  he is watching. He knows my apartment.
One of these mornings he will enter my room.

FLOATING MARKET

Lilit

The bank-brown river slides its skies
down like iridescent silk.
Now blue, now green, it shimmers.
Boats duck their feathers and preen

in it, then crane out their beaks
and bark. We detect no sound,
though we see gems eye their tails
as hucksters turn their boats' stems

upstream, letting the petals
trail bee-bread through the water.
The hucksters' coats are book-blue blots
of the morning's blue. The boats

with their overladen greens,
green-whites, green-yellows, yellows,
and whites are blurred by blue flags
as sleeves wave. The women herd

their hand-picked captives with birds' calls;
they wear palm-leaf hats that cage
their faces in shade; their boats
fleck and minnows of light wade

through their dark unopened smiles.
As they pass, they painfully raise
hands of corpse-ripe fruit. Their arms
wind at the same speed our looks wipe

theirs, as though they were attached
to us by line. From where we watch,
our figures seem to tangle
with a spider's lack of scheme,

but from some point above us,
we mesh like jewelwork, the woof
of what we see happening crossing
the warp of what will never be.

Bangkok, December 1981

WHAT IS WRITTEN IN PORCELAIN

Do not be cold to me. As you press your head
   from me, the air glinting around
  the facets of your face have the crazed
spiderwebbings of fine celadon. Your eyes
  staring hollowly at the sun-drained

corners of rooms are the color of *clair de lune*,
   not blue, not gray. You could glaze
  daylight as it bends by you, so hard
are your gestures; you move with the brittleness
  of shells, give off the jingle of stars

as you want me to leave you. Perhaps the moon
   is made of hoarfrosted ice;
  certainly it is made of frost-white clay
washed with glass. What relationship does it bear
  to you as it floats into the space

behind you sectioned by mullions? The precise
   slant of its blade as it dubs
  your shoulder repeats the reluctance
of your eyes to meet mine. Also, in its strict
  response to the floor through which it stabs

itself, there is much of the same fixed purpose
   with which you break from the room,
  your silks clattering like Imari ware,
the cracked bisque doll beneath that is your body
  unable to contain even my name.

AN ARROW AGAINST EVIL

New Year's Eve.
the cold is rock crystal, which the Chinese name
   "sperm of water" and some still believe
      is petrified ice.
         One man tightrope-walks
a path through the rice-field. Last year's flight feathers
bristle its mirror; they perforate the rime

the moon breathes
on its face. The white-flowering walnut tree's blooms
   tremble as his fingers do inside the two wreathes
      of the rosary
         he is telling. The air
cracks as he cuts through it. He is thinking of the death
of his son. On the right, our joint shadow seems

to be trees
growing tightly together just beyond the frame
   of his vision. Even though he sees
      the steps of the shrine
         washed by the dark waves
of your kimono, the white stones of your heels,
the black stones of mine, rolling beneath as we climb

to the peak
of the hill before him, he will wade the stream
   from our eyes, stave off their wings, and will not speak
      as we lift our bowls
      of New Year's sake

and take the protecting arrows that will fly
straight where our hearts aim them, each to a differ-
ent home.

FORDING THE RIVER

There is no ford here, I can see that,
    but Jong Jin dives the truck in.
Halfway across, the wheels succumb to the soft fruit
    of the bottom. We roll off our socks,
    swing our legs out. The river skewers us
all the way up to the crotch; our toenails wedge
their ice into our toes. Slowly, the water sucks

    the blood from our bones. We push and push,
        the truck will not budge. We race
for the shore, for dry cloths and sunlight. One hour,
    and hour and a half, farmers appear
    to help us. They rock the burrowed truck;
its shell creaks, it sticks its head out. It is beached,
the farmers invite us for fish and fine liqueur.

    The fish is a raw sweetfish, roughly hacked;
        the liqueur is *sochu*, white fire.
The farmers are ancient. Their faces are lined,
    wind-burned. They are my age. I have guessed
    correctly. *Konpei* is a word to know
when drinking. I raise my glass. Here's to the easy life,
here's to our old age, no, youth, *konpei*, a toast!

THE PAGODAS OF PAGAN

Out of the broad brown plain rise a thousand
hives. They are stuck in the tableland at random,
    a vanity full of tarnished silver
perfume bottles. A unity of style tells
    us they are merely the peaks
of a half-buried capital. This winter,
    thoughts of death are a new-built annex:

a dying friend holds me by the hand;
with his eyes I see underground passages,
    with his ears I hear the drone of monks
stocking the dark with endless honey; his feet
    climb with mine the star-scuffed stairs
of pagodas. I would like to think his spirit
    is with me now, will be for years,

but this is illusion. A wasteland
made of time and space has settled between us.
    If I can smell his presence, it is because,
like a long-cherished and obsolete cologne,
    it clings and staggers in tears
down the glossy socket, stronger when released
    here where an eternal city soars.

THE VILLAGE MARKET

Through the awninged walkways the sun's blades
   strike, scissoring into peachgold piles
of mangoes, moongold melons, skingold jackfruit.
The smells from anthills of fresh spices – red, black,
   brown – the smells from spicy smoke, are fused
   with leather, tobacco, fuel oil.
As I near the village square, I am surprised

   by the mellow thock! thock! of a drum:
   not a drum, I see, but stamping stick,
made from two flue-sized lengths of bamboo plunked flat
against the ground. The player is ringed by a crowd,
   and in the center a very old
   woman is dancing. Her moves are stiff
but still graceful. The words of her song are filled

   with minnowy grace-notes. When she sees
   me, she eases into English, "When
was the last time you told me you love me?"
I smile broadly and the crowd laughs. I can read
   in her devious eyes (she has always
   wanted money), the young British soldier
wrapped in her snake-smooth arms, more than her song says.

Pagan, Burma, December 1984

ARRIVING AT MANDALAY

As we leave the boat
between the infantrymen and the stevedores,
  our pretty white man's faces
  draw all the horsecart drivers
  as if by magic.
We choose two of them, delicately scarred.
They lead us to an enamel's gypsy cart,

  pink roses on black.
The stink of sweat and shrimp meal fades. Night parts
  its drapes, plush as painted-tongue.
  The city behind it loafs,
    block after block: parks,
  mansions, markets, villages in parts.
Lights give way to candles, candles to pitch dark.

  When the cart speeds up,
the door claps. When it reels, it sounds like a bar
  being dragged, its flaps swinging.
  The air is oversweet champagne.
    Soon we are drunk on it.
  We pretend we are falling out and laugh.
Suddenly I realize we are running out of map;

  the city blocks sprawl
but they quarter orchards and field. We are out
  in the country. The laughter
  has moved to the front of the cart.

They are taking us
    to a tract where they will rob us and flee.
This fear is a silly fear but it is real.

    "How far is it?" we shout,
for different reasons. There, there around the bend,
    they point, as frightened by our force
    as I was frightened of them.
        After we have dined,
    I am fired by wine to confess my fear.
The fear is gone but the power lasts; I savor it.

A WALK TO SWAYAMBHUNATH

the "Monkey Temple"

One monster eye stares down through the trees
  from the belly of a plaster spire.
"What does the eye mean?" I ask my two small guides,
one twelve, one eight, brothers they say. Buddha sees
    into our hearts. I did not need
a guide. They dogged me down Pig Alley, begging.
  By the time we reached the bridge, their eyes

  had started working in me. They waved
  toward white towers up the valley called
the "Monkey Temple," wouldn't I like to walk
there? Indeed, Buddha does see into our hearts.
  I spin the prayer wheels. I want
my own small boys, ask only to return here.
  Before the clanking stops loneliness starts.

Kathmandu, February 1986

ON THE TRAIN FROM PATNA TO GAYA

An old man made of leather,
  half my size, balances both my bags
on top of his head. His turban keeps them there.
Graceful as a girl on her way to the well
  he wades in front of me. Guidebooks warn
not to travel by night. The train leaves at four.
A woman with baby boards and starts to wail

  just outside my compartment.
  A dark angel in uniform sits
across from me. His smile spreads like a bright knife
or moon slice. I am used to beggars, but he wants me
  to give to her, presses some unknown coins
into my palm. By five o'clock we are still
in the siding. I scowl the sun down through the sky.

  At last we are moving, creaking
  across the rawhide flatness. Handprints
in cow dung cake the farmhouse walls. This is fuel,
but at first I take it for a secret hint
  or greeting, a wave hello! goodbye!
that spreads from yard to yard. By six it is dark.
There are no lights. The darkness grows fluent

  as men climb in the doorways
  when the train slows down. A real moon smiles
from its pond. Moonlight on the dust gleams like salt.
The soldier is silverskinned with it. His arm

moves with a firefly at the end of it
toward my lips. We cannot talk, but we stare, smoke.
I mime a handshake motion. His hands are warm.

A supernova outlines the loved one
  in halo as he comes through the door;
his silhouette, whittled down to melting point
  because the back-light is so sharp,
belongs to any man. Even his clothing,
  linen-white dissolved around his flesh
by the all-consuming aura, begins to warp

  as he comes in. The call, Come to me,
  come, that Godbole sang, echoes here
as the god's figure, dark wick inside the flame,
  ricochets from pane to pane
of the quicksilvery bell-stone. Nosy breathing
  half-disturbs her neck; she turns. His hands,
harsher than a lover's hands should be, dive in,

  and her unmanned parts bristle in ire
  at the unamorous intrusion. She turns
back, and glimpses his face. It is not the face
  of a friend. She has seen men
in all the gods; but, as this godly being
  broods over her and locks looks with her,
he kisses out her cry and his eyes burn.

A YOUNG MASSEUR ENTERS MY ROOM

There is a tap at the door.
  It is furtive, mellow, insistent.
A leather face above its khaki collar
  has the whole moonflowered night
as its nimbus, ten thousand of the moon's arms
  circle from it. He is a soldier
or servant. Panther's muscles rise to the skin and gloat

  just beneath the uniform.
  He waves me toward the bed. I should save
my pride but I am eager to be conquered.
  He pounces, and daggers flare
into my throat. He pounces and kneads
  my crotch. His claws are sheathed in their pads.
As he straddles me to knead my head, I pour

  my fingers across the stones
  in his rump. The lights go out; his skin spills
on me with the sleekness of great cats diving.
  The lights go out; I feel his breath
as he leans across to strike a match. I think
  he is radiating passion or death.
As his eyes pin my eyes on I give off both.

ON VULTURE PEAK

The name comes,
    some say, from the vulture-headed crag
the guide points out, gently tilting me to sight
    the beak, the petrified wings.
Others say that Buddha reached through the mountain
    to calm Ananda, his favorite,
whose stillness was confused by a vulture's fangs.

I see bird,
    where tock is, but I prefer to think
of myself sweating naked in the sun, a hand
    on my shoulder. An old priest
in robes that flow like wine is squatting in a crypt
    with a white boy; they may meditate
there, but this scene is as freehand as a tryst.

If I kissed
    the hem of the priest's skirts, a flowerfest
might shower down, true miracle. I am too crude
    for this holy place; I brood
over a pair of brown and secular bare feet,
    wondering, if I knelt to caress them,
what immediate joy would fall upon my head.

THE EVENING AIR TURNS

When, drunk on treacly Indian rum,
   you plunge into quicksilver
to wash the train ride from Patna from your skin,
fresh linens on the bed will gleam like moonlight
   on milk through the bathroom door.
   Ten minutes will revive you, you think,
as you pour darkly into that tank, the sun

   on your scales glistening in its froth.
   When you wake, the afternoon
is closed for the day. You have lost your chance to tour
the museum. Your belly shines like sari silk
   in the rush-hour light. You stretch,
   reach for the missing body next to yours.
You try to picture the boy in the bazaar

   who courted you. By the time you are dressed,
   cool and white enough for wind
to sift through, the sky is an oilpaper sail
pepper-colored at the edge. The rooftop yard
   of the hotel wears red flowers
   in its hair. Waiters glide through with calls
for whiskey. Outside, the city waits like a bell.

Calcutta, February 1986

FIVE PEOPLE ON A BRIDGE

The river that flows beneath them is the Rhein.
   Above, the sun flows. It carries leaves
      from my heart downstream to them.
   Colors dissolve in it. Minerals
I did not know my blood could bear are leached off
into the current, streaking silver and gold,
silver and gold, like the fluid gilt relief

on a Japanese screen. No one sees the scaled ones
   hanging in the stream behind the paint.
      Why do they swim in the shade
   of the bridge? They do not have ghost fish
hovering under them, their armor does not cast
veils. I am taking the photograph; I stand
slightly upstream in their future. I can taste

with my fins the spine of another bridge arched
   over us. Counting from the left hand,
      four are left. I scan the face
   of the fifth, the last, wondering why death
fell on him, our strongest. Its suddenness crossed
me to the roots. I cling by vein to a brink
in my life, casting leaves, leaves into the past.

ABUSE OF THE SECOND PERSON SINGULAR

We will be remembered for our
   blue pajamas, our lavender
Honey, our vacations
   in Vicenza. Your face fills with milk
As the sun fills its role in your chart,
   but the sky fills with silk

When clouds viciously rip themselves
   across the only limelight
And your face goes dark again.
   Few things on the landscape are as still
As you. The clouds treat you like glass,
   brushing you until you spill

Into the grass, like a delicate
   old claret constantly
Decanted. I have often warned you
   of the danger in this.
I no longer recognize you;
   after years of use you miss

The camera aimed at you. Pictures
   show us pinned beneath the sly
Italian sky, two man-shaped
   patches of blue fallen to earth,
My own face, blotted by leaves,
   robbed of the attention it once was worth.

AN AFTERNOON ALONE

From La Guidecca, the Zattere embankment
seems to salamander along stone, mottled skin
    basking in the sun. This is the back
of Venice. From here the majesty and rot
that shadow the Grand Canal are visible
    only by implication.
    Find an outdoor restaurant and sit

so that necklace of living aquamarines
at your feet will spray diamonds every time
    the city's bosom heaves. Across the silk,
the church of the Gesuati will catch green
from the water and turn to jade. Ask a question
    in Italian so the waiter
    can pour out vowels along with the wine,

either one or both bringing warmth to your glass.
Soon someone will pass and see your silhouette
    pressed like a lover's against the neck
of the harbor. He will turn, join you from the next
table. Behind sunglasses, his eyes will trace
    the blueness or greenness in front
    like lizardskin mirroring its context.

THE GRAND CANAL ON THE MORNING OF THE *REGATA*

If water were music, this river
   would be an aria by Bach,
its soprano brocade underlined
by English horns. Even as the gondoliers' oars
   dip into it, the rich reedy burrs
are set swirling down through the outgoing tide,
threaded with sunlight. The reason that boys choirs

   sound much sweeter in the high voice parts
     is because structures like these,
   the vertical flow of the buildings,
their balconies muffled in frayed velvet swags,
   the monotonous march of the fugues
through the stern chorale, are spiky, masculine,
transparent, but ripe, as though thistles bore figs.

   If all the figures trapped in paintings
     in all the churches were freed,
   the scene would be complete. Modern dress
does not augment it. Only silks and nakedness
   and rags can complement magnificence
and rot, just as Bach's arias thrive on old
throaty instruments and the candor boys possess.

DER ROSENKAVALIER AT THE WIENSTADTSOPER

In anticipation of that rococo jewel chest,
   its autumnal chords silver'd with frost,
    I rush up the steps, push through the crowd.
     The usher has no programs,
wants to sell me a libretto. I refuse
to speak English, half-follow his directions.
Thin whip of a man, I brush the house. My eyes browse,

sipping up the elegance. I flaunt to first row,
   fussing about the schillings I have spent
    to have the first viola stare at me.
     The evening is as much my tale
as it is opera. I dream about myself, dressed
in black and white, against the red dining room.
I taste my loneliness. It should sharpen my feast.

The music box goes on and the drapes go up.
   A kind of wingless angel or god
    sings. Stevens, consume your sour grapes.
     Deny the nightingale's allure.
I would clink my wineglass on yours once, two times,
at intermission, a grandson's kiss. You would find
a program. You could tell me the singers' names.

BOTANICAL GARDEN, SCHÖNBRUNN CASTLE

An old man stops at the bench
where I am sitting, my face
flecking up the mild gold leaf
from the late September sun.
He stands there. "Was duftet so intensive?" he asks.
  He thinks it is juniper, the bush
beside me, bends to burrow in the blue-green mane.

I know what it is. I was drawn
by the scent, sat down. Childhood
favorite, gill-over-the-ground,
not *Waldmeister*, I forget
his word for it so I pick some, bruise its lobes,
  offer its wine to his nose. He smiles
at its sharpness. He recalls that musk underfoot

when he tramped the woods, as I do.
Wohlgeruch, he calls it, perfume.
I settle back, trail my hand
through the stream of consciousness
that flows so freely from my grandparents' world.
  Here, in a world like the world they left,
its old watery colors are not so diffuse.

IT "STANDS FOR ALL THE FABLES OF THE EXOTIC EAST"

The room is bigger than my apartment.
    At the end of an eighteen-hour flight,
I strip in its icebox white, pour a three-shot scotch
    and drink standing in the shower while sweat
        and white-man's stink slide off me.
    A suit the color of *café au lait*
makes me elegant enough to show against the night,

    the palms, orchids poised on smooth brown skin.
    I am alone, but across tablecloths
comes birdsong or laughter bracketed by the clink
    of wineglasses whose notes rise in pitch
        as glasses drain. All other
    diners dine with me. I need not speak;
I need only one of them to want and watch.

Singapore, September 1986

HOW SUNLIGHT IN OUR ROOMS AFFECTS
THE WAY WE SEE THINGS

From the way the sunlight slants
across the floor, I know it is November;
    by the day it overtakes my chair
it will be mid-winter. I guessed what Proust meant,
"the whole world is merely a vast sundial," when I felt
the shadow of the San Marco bell-tower sweep past.
    That was the needle. People who sat

    along the protractor half
of the square were the sundial's ciphers. Camellias
    have begun to bloom. They are set off
by the paleness of the sun, the brief daylight.
My gaze clutches the curtains as though they caught
the features of Venice in their folds. Remnants
    of summer are brought on when the hand-flat

    afternoon slaps these textiles
into motion. Even the moodiest scenes
    are enlivened by its warm infusion.
When Chekhov died, a large black moth, the velvet part
of pansies, flapped through the room. As his corpse cooled,
a bottle of champagne on the night table popped,
    its cork pulled by the sunlight.

BIRD MARKET

Only a Chinese potter
could have confected such glazes:
claire de lune for turtledoves,
sang de boeuf for bowerbirds,
and for the lorikeets Ming dynasty polychrome;
only one very much in love
could arouse such singing:
as I enter their domain,
from every cage they throw their confetti;
trills and turns and mordents sparkle on me.

An amorous fifteen-year-old
smells another man's fiesta on my skin
and clings to me;
he leads me to the bird-of-paradise,
warm-blooded comet,
and in a corner
lit only by that celestial tail
he forms a half-kiss for me.
As psychic as his feathered felons,
he sees through the crystal of my face
a captive face,
blinding as a mask,
wholly occupying me;
he touches me
to appraise the depth of the shadow
and on his fluttering wrist
I feel his song.

A SANCTUARY LINED WITH BATS

This Brahmanical cord,
a Hallowe'en-colored sash
we wind around our waits, will not protect us
from vampire bite. The walls of the grotto pulse
palpably, an undulant of plush,
the swaying grapes of them pursing in and out
through drawstrings at the mouth. They bristle and brush,

their umbrella spokes
or fan sticks so firmly lashed
in silk they only flutter, their natural panache
prepared for nightfall. Close by, they have the lure
of mathematics, vectors in flesh
converging on a face. As I reach to touch
the lush and lustrous velvet, their eyeteeth gnash

and a skirl goes up
along the arbor. The guide hauls
my hand down and holds it down. How he holds it
is cat's-paw around a pounce, the polished steels
inside the smooth skin wound and set to flash.
This is a holy place; the bats are holy.
He joins his palms and prays. I pray, too, or wish.

TURNING NORTH

As the Southern Cross slides down and off,
    your land fades silver and out of sight
by fisher-fire and runway light. You watch the sky
    a while, then you turn to face the road
    and suddenly wave for a *becak*.
Into the slow spin of your city the wheels
    whisper. They whispered the night before,
    whispered with rain, the slick of the street
pulled momently before falling, as I held your hand
down, down between my legs so hard your skin broke.
    Now you sit with your hands to one side,

    both palms up, their lifelines blacking out
    in curls of shadow as one by one
the streetlights are passed. My own hands are clasped hard
    between my legs in prayer or witchcraft,
    weird enough to turn, turn the plane around
from a land I do not love back to your land.
    I ride where you ride, live the dark
    that even now deepens in the house
where you are going, though the plane is in a zone
above that dark. And one hour and one sky away
    the plane burns with me and stays aloft.

GECKO HOUR

There is a mood, here in the tropics, as night falls,
    that settles over us in long folds
with its purples and its golds and we swamp with peace.
We are sitting on the balcony watching lights
    come on in cross-cut all over town;
or we are looking down across pagoda flowers
    at rice fields filling with firefly sparks,
watching John sway up with drinks as the sun wanes;
or in a café at one of the Raffles parks,
    counting the gecko's strokes as day
strikes six and seeing, really seeing, the blooms alight
    on the plumerias, white on white.
It might be fair, the air brut and bubbly and cool,
or it might be raining; but if it rains, it rains
thunderous with applause and fire-wild for a while.

I try to bring this mood back, back into these walls
    with me, back into a land I do not love.
It holds as long as my heart holds up, then it folds
and flags in the rain. I sit smoking, the door left
    open to the night, and the scent of cloves
reeks back to me. There are roses out there, bowers
    with knots of red and white with brown marks
on them, all rotted by the rain. It rains and rains
and the roots of the roses are drowning in it. The rain barks
    by day and bays by night. Gray and gray
deafens all the greens, dulls the light from edge to edge,
    even in the house. Hydrangeas wedge

their way up, gorged on the rain. Their blue-gray cloth
matches the swag of southern flowers. But the rain
is chill and carries in with it drags of death.

AMOROUS THOUGHTS IN THE SURGING WAVE PAVILION GARDEN

It is summer, and the mean wear shorts.
   Nothing could distract my sight
   from the irregular smooth line
of the jigsaw stone path and its bamboo fence.
   To the twenty-year-old in white
walking with his right hand gliding along the rail,
there was nothing eventful about the afternoon
   until my eye caught him. As a horse
   twitches its neck to release a fly,
he twitched his back. He tugged on my flourish of thoughts,
   bird-of-paradise spraying sunshine

   behind it. The long buffalo horns
    of the Mountain-View Tower gored
    the sky from a feathery mane
of bamboo. It was a place to stop and talk.
   He was willing. He played kite
to my twine, always blossoming as his skin
slid up and down along his spine. Around the bend
   he disappeared. He was in his seat,
   waiting for me. I knew. Now my hand
held itself up by holding the fence. I walked
   by sense of touch, exactly as though blind.

THOUGHTS OF OLD AGE AND DEATH IN WANGSHI GARDEN

It is too easy to say
that my life, like the Meandering Corridor,
    zigs and zags without intent; a rock
(once, a country; another time, a stray event)
    turns its course from right to left.
    Without intent but not without design:
    not until the farther wall is reached
does the tree-like twist, as logical in blueprint
as one brushstroke in a great unfinished word,
    make sense; close by , the rock had to be
    immovable, a given element,

    but plans from the early Ch'ing
show in that place: nothing. The spring winds semaphore
    by branch beyond the hollow window,
a reckoning of green and white. This is meant
    for me. They urge me to rest
    a while. Ten years, twelve years, I have done it once
    and once too often. Beauty is blamed
for being covert and conniving, but this complaint
is of the heart. Old age is the surrender
    to the purposelessness of life, awake
    at last when too many years were spent.

THE BLUE MOSQUE

We pass into a galaxy of cornflowers.
The architectural lining is drenched in blue:
    phlox blue, parrot blue, robe-of-Mary blue.
The eye is caught in a filigree of brier-rose
        that no prince will penetrate,
shatters as it climbs, climbs the rafterless roof
    into clustered cupolas. We stand
    in an acre of marble rain forest;
the breaks between the boughs are sunned through wind-chimes
    of the thinnest blue glass. Though no blue
is bluer than the blue of the tiles, a new blue blooms

where light falls: eye-white behind iris blue sours
into the blue whey of milk; the darkest hues
    go purple. The holy space is halved
into a more holy space and a less holy space
        by a fence; we are on the half
where the dark bloods of carpets effloresce the miles
    of naked or nearly-naked feet
    that trample them each day. As we watch
the shadows drop, caught in the cross-fire of God,
    their outlines blue with fire, an effect
of backlight. I want to be on the other side.

ACROSS THE REDLANDS

As we drive and drive,
we see we are scaling an underwater ridge.
   The first stage from Waingapu goes flat,
the road a welt across an abyssal plain
that is now near bare; from time to time a gap
   the jeep drives through has a sudden grove
   that shades a shack or shelters a few cows
tied to thorn brush. Grasses, too, rage out in these rifts
      through crustings of coral and ferns
   furrow through clefts, anywhere once wet.
After an hour we are striving a spine,
staring down into trenches and fosses furred
   with an even green. It is clear from here
how sea floor builds up, layer by layer, the ruts
between the wales making ribbed velvet of it.

Sun gods and rain gods
war constantly as we cross, changing the sky
   for us between one pass and the next pass.
Brazen blue is chased by a shatter of spray
that pebbles the windshield. We stop at a break
   in this, at a stirrup in the road
   where cassias flirt their yellow at us.
In this high place, at sheet-cloud range above the hills
      with their cascades of rice fields
   there in the valley, the earth is red
with coral dust. We have found the mother of this dust,
delicate shrubs of it, down there on the beach.

"Treasure," you called it. For me the prize
was to have you with me again, to travel
as far and almost as fast as we once did.

PASSING BY OUR OLD APARTMENT

Up the hill I walk,
    up the street that was a dream I had,
a street I thought was San Francisco. I move
by rote from light to light, casting no shadow,
    haunting my own past. We left
this world, you to the east and I to the west,
    but our life here is still felt
in the worlds where we are. I step where darkness stalls,
not wanting to be seen as a stranger here,
    but coming home. I look up and see
    the *shoji* is open, a light on
in the inner room. A shadow streams and falls
on the window and a face looks down at me.

That face is your face,
    so strong do I long for it. I am mad,
I know, but I want to go up there and prove
it is you, walk inside, into the hollow,
    up the fire escape, turn left,
and open the door. Our years here were not the best
    years of our lives, but wounds melt
at the sight of you, this one sight of you calls
me back to this world with you. I was not one
    to want you here. But now, as I rove
    off again to where you have not gone,
I know that those years with you, right within these walls,
was the only time in my life I ever was in love.

UP IN FLAMES

Twelve rooms in this house,
    a Christmas tree in every room, a tree
in every corner of the hall, this is the way
    to be festive. Always underfed,
    I haunt the dining room for festoons
above my head. Someone is there I need to know,
    across the white damask, across the flint
    of the crystal, across the dull smart
of the silverware. I reel him in by eye
and he says he knows me. We are at the height
    of the dance when his woman friend moves in
    and he moves away. My personal space
shrinks as she backs me toward the wall; I hardly fit

between the hall stand
    and the sideboard. There are candles on fire,
candles on fire everywhere, huffing at us.
    My bulky sweater billows with heat.
    As the woman talks, my forehead faints
toward her. There is a ring of warmth in my back
    that is growing sharp, and a smell so sharp
    I shudder at it. I turn to look
in the hall stand mirror and see that I am on fire
and smoke is pouring up. I start to beat at it
    with my hands and the young man comes in
    and beats it out and holds my arms hard
and looks at me. The real fire is in my heart.

JOURNEY UP THE GYAING

From left bank across to right bank it runs down
molten glass. Where it meets the Salween, that Roman Road
from the north, it roils and seethes, finally cools,
its melt taken by spin into the great thresh
thudding and undertowing off toward the sea.
We are only a skim on its glare. The hull
is burning around us. The flat is so hot
that it reflects nothing: palms weep over by root
from the mud without casting the slightest ghost
on it; looking down into what would be tuff
if it set, I see only a breath of my face,
your face, marbling the smoke. My breast fumes and sweats.
You touch me and your handprint is white and wet

on my skin, proving that I am already burned,
and nothing more. I have your head in my hold
so hard, hoping to break your mouth in on my neck,
I feel the drum shape beneath your scalp. I have sparred
with you, watching your gaze go wide as my strokes
reached for the tacit agreement of your sex,
broke on your fist, and fell, so I turn this flirt
into a joke. Soldiers on the shore see two forms
fold from me as I give birth to you. We nest
in the scull, craning out at some other prey
in the soldierly shadows. Every mile we ride,
upriver, downriver, is one more mile for me
closer to the night when you will drown in my arms.

TO THE FARM CAVES

Dead flat the sun smashes on our head
and shoulders. The "road" he promised is dike
   between rice fields that we thread. Some men
have a name for this that means hard on bare feet,
   small sharp stones and halancing, arms out.
There are rainbows there at times between the stubs,
   whatever makes them, and darts at the roots
that are tiny eels, but mostly it is the sun,
   "day's eye" they call it, the sun grown hard
and thick skimming through a mere slick, following us
   field to field. The blue of the sky eats

   at us. No hats, no water to drink,
we lapse into pools of shade whenever we can.
   After every few hours of such sun
a man's spine churns up into his brain a cloud
   they sat is madness. Now I am mad,
and when we reach the miracle village I slump
   and hobble to the nearest sill, "Go on
without me." There are no horse carts up ahead,
   I no longer believe this young man,
though he pray me. If I die now, they will bear me
   to the head man's hut and lay me down

   on clean mats, and he will pray for me,
and they do, the one I love taking most of my weight
   onto his slender shoulders. Five cups
of Chinese tea and I am right again. They prowl

around us at first, think CIA;
they have never seen white men, only on TV,
    but soon I am someone to smile with.
They invite us to rest, and we go inside.
    This is what I wanted, lying here
in the near dark, next to him, if only his words
    are not by heart, and not by word of mouth.

WOLF HOUR

Winter, and wolf hour
is that time beyond sunset when shadows stretch
    and reach for you and you drown in them.
      I would sit, fixed to my chair,
    as the dark hunkered down and stalked me.
Mother would come into the room and find me there,
    shuddering, two big hull's-eyes in my face,
    and she would switch on a lamp and light
would sweep and the beast would run and hide from her.
    Summer nights came differently, the black
settled on each branch of the sky, its feather weight

letting out the fire
though its eyes. I could stand it, stand and let its gaze
    drizzle over me. For years I forgot
      wolf hour, forgot how the webs
    would gather into a shape and stalk me,
standing so close I felt the brunt of its stare,
    I felt its huff on my hands. My life
    is back where it was – winters are cold
and I am afraid of them. When wolf hour comes
    I sit and wait it out, wait for the dark
to struggle it, and I am lonelier than a child.

AS IN A PAINTING BY FÜSSLI

At night the heaviness comes.
A nightmare sits my chest and picks my bones. Owl
    or moloch, the creature feeds on me
        and my heart skitters its hole,
blood beating. This summer, two friends died, first one
    and then the other. May, and we knew
the one was ill, but by midsummer, his friend,
    the sound one – or so we said – was gone,
    the tramp cells run wild around his lungs.
They were old men, yes, but strong (that was last year),
    and now I wake at three o'clock and feel
the same death thrill all through me. Death was a door,
I thought, open or shut, built of steel and stone.

    Now I see it as a scrim,
thinnest of possibilities, draped through my room
    at night. I feel it next to me. My hand
        is touched by wind from behind,
or breath, and I fear that it will have me
    unless I turn and hug away as far
as I can. But there is no one to cling to.
    My powers have grown since I reached my own
    dark side of life. The one power I fear
is the power to trade across death's door new souls
    for old, or old for new. There is one love
over there I do not dare to long for here
for anyone. Or the next death may be mine.

VIEW OF THE RIVER

My last day here and for once
I shake off the sway of the land and stroll down
   to where my field ends ragged in ash
and asters at the edge of the neighbor's lawn.
   There a haven opens up to me.
   This is the view I am toiling to take
   for my own land, a bench here, a grove
of rhododendrons all around, tamarisks
on the right to break the upright of the trees,
rosebay on the left, the whole window a case
   with whatever frame I make for it.
This summer, a flock of artists perched in this field
      to paint. I have a masterpiece

      here – Corot, the way my eyes
see it – yet I never make time to sit and gaze
   at it. The sun flows now in a flash
as the tide comes in. The greens around are drawn
   into that radiance. There is no way
   to blind the beholder. Flake by flake
   of flake white might suggest it, a cove
compacted with brilliants and chrome green with whisks
of Naples yellow in it for grass. My home
is here. I long for the time I can stay, held
   by this view down between the lilacs
I just planted, so sweet to be at rest at last
      but bitter because I am old.

THE DEER DRINK AT OUR POND

They must have been watching from our woods,
their taste for our water sharpening as I dug,
    the trench lengthening day by day
    until that thirty-foot dark was deep
    and could hold it all, sweet, bright,
for the evening I put in place the last sod,
    gazing at that span plated by the sun,
devil's darning needles already threading it,
    they came down and drank from it
    as I left, stag, doe, two fawns,
    the hoods of their eyes lowered as they bent
    to face the gold. After that they came
each evening. I would find hoofprints in fresh mud

    in the morning. The cat, too, learned to drink
from it, pausing in her hunt to cling to the turf
    at the edge of it, her paw thrust
    into it from time to time to test
    what it was. She was drawn first
by the shimmer. I waded through it to hoist
    water lilies in and the whole sheet shook.
By summer's end, time to leave, the plantings held,
    started growth. Next year the grass
    should be thick enough to mask
    the hoofprints of the deer by the time
    I push my way through winter, through spring,
toward summer, toward my homeland, to quench my thirst.

WIND FROM THE WEST

It comes, comes down from the hills,
and dries, dries the land, dries up the roots of things,
    then moves on, on toward the sea.
    The earth is powder in my hand;
    it winnows away from me, dead dry.
    The waxbells I brought with me stand and flag,
missing their homeland wet, their maple leaves scuffed flat
    by the wind. Out in the field
the poplars flag, too, as the west walks through them,
    their cash jingling bright at the edge of pines.
Only plants that thrive on scree show through, their wealth spilled

    in reds and purples down rift
and overhand, a pennyworth, though, against vast browns.
    The rest of the garden sickens me.
    One week left before I leave,
    one week to save the summer's handiwork,
    what in my mind were drifts and spires and swag
moving between the lawns now tattered and buffed
    there where brambles still hold ground.
For I go back west, that west beyond the west
    that is East for us, where loneliness blows
and howls through all my nights, harsher than the wind.

WE VISIT THE SON OF THE LAST SHAN PRINCE

Horst swerves his lens toward the house,
  the "palace," and a hand waves him down,
    a voice scolds him off. Our host
calls us down out of earshot, down to the pool,
    and there he rants and rankles at the State,
the Union. They are not his folk. He would still make
prince were it not for those barbarians. The pool cracks
with weeds, unused to water, no longer stage
    for any swimming thing. We stare inside
as he speaks, all three of us, summoning a show
    from the twenties. He likes riddles. "That pipe,"
he points to the roof, "What is it for?" Its steam
    signaled to those on the tennis court
that hot water was now ready for their bath.
Grandfather, an Oxford man, designed a home

    for the lush life. As we roam
    amidst the ancient appointments that crown
    the place, the might-be prince may boast
a little too much about their rise and rule
    here, but we marvel that the same rich fate
that takes over the fields did not overtake
the house. He shows us inside a home of wax
in photographs: Grandfather at every age,
    then Father and Father's Austrian bride.
They met in Colorado. She did not know
    he was a prince. We sit for a tintype
of ourselves, so still that the shadows do not seam

our clothes. They would serve tea but the fire is out.
We are steeped in story and stay in its aftermath
a while as light seeps out and we turn monochrome.

Burma, December 1999

I WILL NOT SEE THE SNOW THERE THIS YEAR

While I was shivering all night
    in the train down through the mountain range
    from Lasho to Mandalay, eighteen hours,
snow was whisking in from Canada in drifts
around our house. You were warmer inside, the air
    scented with balsam fir, the white dusk
    inlaid with the same small colored lights
we often see in the arches around the Buddhas here,
    than I was, warmer than I was
    even after the sun rose and the train
    started its zig-zag down toward the plain
    and stopped for a while and vendors came
to the windows and I had hot tea. Your fire

    was hotter than the sun at noon
    in that high city at the gateway
    to China. Wave after wave of chill
whirred through me that day as we shopped the bazaar
for Christmas gifts. I thought of you the night before,
    gathered in front of that fire, champagne
    icy in fluted glass, all the flair
and flourish I renounced this year. I was cold
    until we were out of the hills.
    The deer came right up and left slim trails
    near the door, you said. That was the day
    we rode elephants, great and gray
and never to be missed, though delicately belled.

BE HE ALIVE OR BE HE DEAD

A giant is sleeping under our pines.
   I have noticed there are spates
in the forest where no one walks. The old ones
in blue out collecting mountain pepper skirt
   these places. The snorts I hear at night
   are not the earth stretching or the house
      dead on its feet – my worst fears
   so far – but something far less understood.
Yes, it is Hallowe'en, and something is out there.
I am not mad, but I hear hills hackle up
at night and scratch their shapes on my windows.
   I will not go out. I let my dreck
pile up – newspapers, shoes, the break-ups and burrs

   of things – until the rooms ache to hold
      it all. People pass and ask
if anyone lives there – here; blind as my house
I hide in the afternoons of all my days,
   coming to light only when they sleep.
   It is my craziness that keeps me.
      If I lived as long as they all live,
   flat-faced, mountainous and without end
in their lack of sympathy, I would be dead
by now. Oh, but I am dead, dead to this world,
this world of little men. They say a giant sleeps
   beneath the pines (judging from his dregs).
But they mean me and they mean lying in my grave.

HOME FOR CHRISTMAS

This is your family and no,
I am not part of it. Custom runs
so by clockwork that even though someone dies
it all goes on – carols play, fires light,
champagne pours – it all goes on once more.
I smell the sharp oil as the wheels turn.
We stand here and there and the flash
welds us into one group. But no, I am not part of it.
I am not part of it. I sit off
to one side and feel the day flow by
and know I am not part of it. There is a hush

in the room as the clocks chime
and the time for the children to come
comes. Voices cross in the doorways and the halls,
calling each other across the years,
but they do not call to me. I sit
off to one side in the red/green chill
of Christmas lights, but their power
does not touch me. The group moves in for the cheer
and glasses hand around. I cleave to my chair,
remembering how the drinks would make their way
in my family, how quick we were
to reach for them, but always with a touch of fear.

HOW TO CONJUGATE THE VERB "*AIMER*"

When you had your womanhood ripped out
of you, you slumped in the drift snow of your bed
and watched videos, their colors splaying out
    across the starched whites around you, life
        projected onto you. One
of these you sent to me, "amused" by it
you said. It was a French film about two men
(I forget the name), one clever (that was me),
    the other Mongoloid (but was that *him*?
    For when you spoke of him, a blur or gloss
spread over your face that was meant to mean "I love
    you both"). This tense is the *parfait*.
We met because I was invited to live

    in your country, hole up in your lair,
shower my genius on you. And this I did,
at lunch or over coffee. The rest of the time
    you hunched in front of the screen, wave on wave
        of data pouring over you.
Eventually all of it made its way
into your thesis, weeded by your comments.
Reading it, I found little of my effect
    on you. And this is the *pluparfait*.
    And then here you came, came to Japan,
came to live with me a while, the daughter (or niece)
    I never had. And I made plans,
plans, reading into the lift of your voice a trace

104

of bond. But as I summered at home,
you wound your way into my house, broke your trust
and loosed your friends inside. Nothing much was brashed
   but our feelings flew across a half world
      faster than our words could flash
along the keys. And I returned and found walls healed,
windows cured, chairs corrected. What was not repaired
was love. Love! – the last word that you said to me
   (but from your blind). This is the *imparfait*.
   And what of the *présent*? There is no news.
You might be in Moscow, you might be in Mainz,
      You might be in Monterey.
I learned you had left from Ikeda's complaints

   about your flight. My neighbor, your "friend" –
a piece of local color acquired by you –
he knew only that you wanted to be home
   by Christmas and you never called to say
      goodbye. But why would you call?
And what is meant by "home"? And so I bang and bang
at your old advisor for some key to you.
He says simply, "She loves you." But as I pare
   this contradiction down he swats and shoos
   me off, his huff honeyed with the proof
that your new book bears in its preface a fanfare
   of thanks to me. But by now my heart
can filter out the past. This verb has no *futur*.

THE AFTERNOON SESSION RUNS OVERTIME

You and I sit perched on the sills of our chairs
as the Q & A edges five minutes, ten, fifteen
  into *my* time. Three professors stand
in front haranguing the young contestant; he fends
  off their attack and seems to dread not,
though the red is rising to his face. Two of the pugs
  who dod him are old, creaking; the third,
in the center, has just fired his masterwork,
  a dictionary, at us and is full
of fettle; his Russian glints in the broadsides of sun
  that slant through the room and consonants hurl

  at his opponent, slicing through the pith
of his defenses. This presentation has turned
  into a springboard for a monologue
by each of these three. At last the young man retreats,
  sits, and by this I know it is my turn.
We spring into action, distribute the handout
  as far as it will go (for the room has filled),
you on the one side, I on the other, and though I should feel fear,
  following this foray, I feel more
your support sustain me, and as I pass out
  my share I pause at the young man, smile
and wink, almost flirt with him. Up front I calm
  and fill with confidence. Attention is whole

  as my sweet English sweeps along the ears
of the audience and my glance roves here and there

over the faces focused on me.
This is success! The king of the conference sits
    immediately behind you, and as I spot
back to that hub it is your look I see, not his,
    and my pride is much more in your gift
for interacting with these people (better than I do)
    than in my own bravura. We smile
at the end. There are few comments. Even the bugbear,
    who knows this subject best, smiles and is still.

Moscow, July 2005

DANCING ABOARD THE SUNBOAT III

There are four of us "old" men. A Nubian dance troupe
    (all men) have come to entertain us.
They start off in groups of four, five, six, the rest
    clapping is time as the young men swag,
the forms beneath the *gallabiyas* seduced

by the ardor of the beat into swirls and sweeps,
    the drape of the cloth caught on some plane
momently of bone beneath. And then they break
    into a line dance, invite us to join.
The woman do, then one younger man. The two others seek

support and they too join in. A flare of hands
    as Andrew (one of us four) steps out
into the round. You look at me; you know how much
    I like to dance (or did) and just how well.
A ringleader drags at my hand. Soon I am a match

for most of them: sway, kick, sway, kick, turn, sway, kick.
    The music is our jolt and we jaunt
back and forth, heads swirling, gasping for breath. A lull,
    and in that lull I see one man urge
at you to dance with us. But you sit bolt still,

hands braced into the sofa. No one would guess,
    from what they must take to be a lack
of skill or simply shyness, how well you waltz.
    I used to watch at weddings from the wings
and I wished I could dance there with you. Not much else

is denied to us. In Vienna, on New Year's Eve,
    I once wanted to waltz the night away.
But that will never be. You sit still and stare
    and the stiffness there is in your heart,
thoughts of dancing with us fanning a flame of fear.

Aswan, March 2006

AT ABU SIMBEL

The *colossi* tower above us,
not reaching sky but seeming to support it,
    as planned, unobscured by haze
    in the dearth of this land. From where we stand,
at the toe of the scalene triangle whose leg
is the slope of the temple front, the slant side
is our line of sight along Rameses' beard
    and the spine of his nose; his eyes clear
    this segment, staring beyond survey
into endlessness. As we enter the throat
    of the sanctuary, an aura foams
around us, either aftershock of the sun
or the wake of spirits. O Pharaoh, you stand today

    in multiple here because the world, informed
with this spirit, sent men who with certainty and skill
    block by block, slate by slate, sawed through
    the stone and, lifting each numbered piece
in order into place, rebuilt your temple sound
on higher ground, making up a mountain around it
as site. Meanwhile in other lays of the land,
    men with minds made of mud have been
    blasting buildings down. Yes, we have powers
greater than yours, to preserve or destroy
    the world. "O Ozymandias, King of Kings,"
some day some man may stand here and dwell on this:
That your realm lasted much longer than did ours.

WHY THE WORD "HOMESICK"
CAN NOT BE TRANSLATED

It comes from the outcast, this impulse to go back,
from Oedipus at Thebes, at home yet not at home,
the mind with its eyes out by the power of will
suddenly beckoned through the heart with needles
of light. Imagine how, in his innocent
delight, in the lush embrace of his mother,
an unexplained lethargy might honeycomb

his flesh, making him gag on her and roll
leadenly from her powerfully perfumed side.
How he must have clawed the air as that other face,
that Ginevra de' Benci face, not wholly
beautiful but genuinely motherly,
swam beneath the Comedy mask that confused
the mother's features worn by his new-won bride,

as the fish's shadow underlines the fish.
There was the real incest, that wish for the hands
from childhood we call "home." The exile has no right
to remember. He must be blind. He must mute
his breast, suffocate the hint of the scent of thyme
his feet used to bruise as he turned in at the gate,
as he treads forever the walks of foreign lands.

ABOUT THE AUTHOR

Roger Finch was born in Pittsburgh in 1937, graduated with a B.A. in Music Theory from The George Washington University, and subsequently received a doctorate in Near Eastern Languages and Literatures from Harvard. In 1977 he moved to Japan and began teaching at Sophia University and Waseda University in Tokyo; currently he is Professor at Surugadai University in Saitama Prefecture. He has published two previous collections of poetry, *According to Lilies* (Carcanet, 1992) and *Foxin the Morning* (Leviathan, 2000).

From Roger Finch's long experience of living in Japan and traveling widely in the Far East, Europe, and other countries come the settings and themes of many of these poems dealing with love and friendship, encounters with strangers, discovery, loss, and death, while others focus on memories of the past, separation, and longing for his homeland. The prosodic base of most of these poems is that of syllable count, inspired by that of Japanese, Korean, Thai, and Quechua poetry, and they are often colored by subtle "cumulative" rhymes involving the last accented syllable of three lines in each stanza.

Made in the USA
Monee, IL
07 July 2026